How the British came to Bordigh on the Italian

by Carolyn McK

Introduction

A 19th century British winter – it meant at best short, damp days, often shrouded in fog; at worst soot-laden air and bronchial ailments. For the well off, escape to a sunny, coastal winter resort was an option – Nice, Cannes and Menton on the French Riviera were popular destinations although by the mid-1800s they were becoming rather crowded, fairly socially demanding and somewhat more expensive than when they were first established. When John Ruffini's unassuming little book entitled *Doctor Antonio* was published in Edinburgh in 1855 it must have been exactly what many of its winter-bound readers had been waiting for.

As winter closed in, there was comfort and inspiration in reading about an as yet undiscovered place abroad where the climate was milder, the air was so much cleaner, and the surroundings were rural and charmingly rustic. So much so that from 1855 to around 1935 the story of Bordighera's growth and development reads like a *Who's Who* of the British upper class. More than 150 years since the first winter "settlers" arrived, the town's British heritage is still remembered and commemorated in its tennis courts, its Anglican church, its international library and museum. In *How the British came to Bordighera on the Italian Riviera* I explore this unusual aspect of Bordighera's history. I have not attempted to write a comprehensive guide to modern Bordighera, but at the end of *How the British came to Bordighera on the Italian Riviera* I have included some hints to help you plan a visit.

How the British came to Bordighera on the Italian Riviera

Spring 1819, a short distance east of Bordighera on the recently built Grande Cornice Road linking Genoa to Nice.

The road is rutted and dusty and while neither particularly steep nor winding at this point it is perilously narrow. The humble cart jolts its two passengers along. The older man would doubtless prefer to be travelling in more style, but the boy, eleven or twelve years old, is oblivious to both discomfort and hazards. He loves it when his uncle takes him along on his trips to Ventimiglia.

He's enchanted by the steep terraced hillsides that rise above the road on his right: olive trees thrive here along with palms, lemons, grapes and figs and the varying greens and greys of foliage and bark paint an image in his mind that will never fade. He peers with awe at the olive groves and remembers how just a few years ago a pack of wolves ventured out of the hills right down to the town gates. Are they even now still lurking there, watching them pass, he wonders.

Giovanni's uncle lives in Taggia, an inland town some 30 kilometers to the west. The boy is boarding there in order to complete his education. He wishes Taggia were on the coast, like the small town they are approaching now - then his school days would be perfect.

If, looking down to his left, young Giovanni is tempted to inch closer to his uncle and grip the rail of the cart for safety, he shows no sign of apprehension. Beyond the edge of the road it's a sheer drop into the sea. Giovanni wriggles with excitement.

There'll be pirates and smugglers hiding in the stony coves, he muses, and maybe mermaids just below the surface of the water. Ahead of them now stretches a sea-green expanse of flat land. They have reached the outskirts of Bordighera and are descending into a vast plantation of palm trees. All around them palm fronds wave gracefully beneath a clear blue sky. Emerald green and sky blue: another image that Giovanni will never forget.

Giovanni and his uncle alight from the cart at the post chaise station in Bordighera. It's a small village of fishermen and farmers, occupying a fortified headland and the land sloping down to the harbour. Around the headland olive and citrus groves flourish and magnificent palm plantations add an exotic touch. In many respects – apart from the date palms – it is typical of many another village along the Ligurian coast: Ventimiglia, Ospedeletti, Sanremo, Riva, Santo Stefano, San Lorenzo, San Maurizio,

Cervo ... all of them are similar; in the early 1800s they offered the traveller – since the term *tourist* didn't really apply – rudimentary comfort. The notion of their villages being *attractions* in themselves for wealthy foreigners was practically incomprehensible.

Giovanni Ruffini, born in Genoa in 1807, would in fact later describe Bordighera as his *first flame*, and those scenes from his trips with his uncle, kept alive in his memory, would one day be put to a use that the enraptured boy could never have imagined.

By 1830 Ruffini had graduated in Law from Genoa University. The Italian peninsula - at that time still a collection of kingdoms, dukedoms, Papal States and a colony of the Austrian-Hungarian Empire – was beginning to ferment. Although it would be a good 30 years before these components began to be unified as the Kingdom of Italy, the Resurgence – *Il Risorgimento* – was well under way. Nationalist sentiments had been astir since Napoleon's rule ended in 1815. As a youth, Ruffini became interested in the concept of unification and befriended fellow Genoan and avid political activist, Giuseppe Mazzini. Mazzini had been arrested in 1827 for his involvement in an unsuccessful secret pro-unification movement, and following his release in 1831 had gone into exile firstly in Switzerland, and later in Marseilles in the south of France. Here he founded a new movement called *Young Italy*: by 1833 there were about 60,000 sympathizers including Giovanni Ruffini and his brothers Agostino and Jacopo. Since the Congress of Vienna in 1815, the region of Liguria – with Genoa as its capital and including Taggia and Bordighera - had been incorporated in the Kingdom of Sardinia and ruled by the House of Savoy. Mazzini's vision of creating a united republic, and the insurrections he organized from Marseilles to this end, were therefore acts of treason, which, when discovered led to numerous arrests, imprisonments and executions. In fact, Jacopo Ruffini's arrest and subsequent suicide in prison in 1833 led to Giovanni and Agostino Ruffini joining Mazzini in exile in Marseilles. From here they moved to Switzerland and on to England in 1837.

Giovanni Ruffini, Cape Ampelio Gardens, Bordighera

In London a series of events led to the beloved Bordighera of Giovanni Ruffini's childhood becoming an amazingly popular British winter destination. His enthusiasm for Mazzini's political notions waned and he took a more moderate stance on the approach to unification. He dedicated a great deal of time to perfecting his grasp of English and began to write in that language. His first novel, *Lorenzo Benoni*, was published to great acclaim in Edinburgh in 1853. In this largely autobiographical work he introduced his readers to the lot of those who were struggling to procure the peninsula of Italy's unification and freedom from foreign powers: an account of patriotic sentiments, secret societies and insurrections. Like Ruffini's own life, *Lorenzo Benoni* ends with Benoni's flight into exile in 1833. The success in Britain of *Lorenzo Benoni* soon had Ruffini's publisher asking for a sequel. However Ruffini was unable to write it: his loss of interest in

Mazzini's movements had left him disinclined to continue Benoni's story. Instead, Ruffini's friend and fellow writer, Henrietta Jenkin, took up the story and wrote a novel relating an Italian exile's life: *Who Breaks – Pays*, published in 1868. As with the autobiographical *Lorenzo Benoni*, Henrietta Jenkin drew on her own experiences to spice up *Who Breaks – Pays*. Agostino Ruffini had been her lover while her husband was posted abroad: later Giovanni would become her lover while he was living in Paris with another English writer, Cornelia Turner.

Although Mrs. Turner, who was more than ten years Ruffini's senior, was estranged from her husband, Ruffini claimed to regard her as a mother figure.

Whatever the finer details of this trio's relationship, affection and collaboration were undoubtedly among the sentiments that they shared. Even if neither Henrietta Jenkin nor Cornelia Turner had been published when Ruffini decided to tell his story in *Lorenzo Benoni*, it seems inevitable that they would have assisted him with the mechanics of writing the novel in English for a British market. When he did write a second novel, again in English, the two women were doubtless Ruffini's literary mentors and linguistic guides. In spite of their probably not inconsiderable contribution however, only one name – John Ruffini – features on the cover of *Doctor Antonio*, published in Edinburgh in 1855.

Opening in western Liguria in early spring, 1840, against a backdrop of the unification movement, *Doctor Antonio* is a poignant blend of romance, patriotic pride, armchair travelogue and local history guide. Drawing on Ruffini's childhood memories of the trips he had made along the coast with his uncle, the novel begins on the Grande Cornice Road.

However it is no humble cart that we see in the opening pages but rather the elegant carriage of a haughty, middle-aged English Lord, Sir John Davenne. He is travelling from Rome back to England with his invalid daughter, Lucy. Normally such a journey was made by ship since travelling by road was extremely slow and uncomfortable. The wolf packs that young Giovanni Ruffini remembered were not the only danger lurking in the hills: bandits were constantly on the lookout for unwary victims. As well, the road itself was in places little more than a ledge cut into the mountainside, with a steep cliff on one side and a sheer drop down on the other.

Faced with these discomforts, few Grand Tourists would have actually chosen to travel overland, in spite of the lush vegetation and fragrant aromas that Ruffini describes in chapter one.

As often happened though, stormy seas and Lucy's poor health had forced the Davennes to disembark in La Spezia after only a few days at sea and continue by carriage. Sir John's servant, John Ducket, and Lucy's maid, Miss Hutchins, are travelling in the rumble seat. Prospero, the young Italian postilion, having taken on a fifth horse in Sanremo in order to hasten their progress, is now, in the descent into Bordighera, struggling to retain control of the carriage and horses. Realizing that he cannot reign the horses in to the sedate pace required as the road slopes down to the harbour, Prospero decides to let them choose their own speed: he will slow them again when they reach the flat land along the shore. Unfortunately Sir John becomes alarmed at the carriage's reckless speed and shouts to Prospero. Lucy screams and Prospero is distracted for the few seconds it takes for the carriage to skid on a stone and topple over – luckily they have almost reached the shore and the conveyance quickly slithers to a halt on a sandy slope. Only Lucy is badly hurt – her leg is broken just above the ankle. While John Ducket examines the damage to the carriage, Prospero stands gaping at the scene in a daze. As Sir John and Miss Hutchens gather around Lucy, a gig pulls up and out hops Doctor Antonio.

There is something of Giovanni Ruffini in this efficient and charming doctor, since like Ruffini, he is also a political exile – this time from his native Sicily.

In the opening chapters of *Doctor Antonio*, Ruffini wastes no time establishing a trusting and affectionate relationship between Antonio and Lucy. Gaining Sir John's confidence is a much harder task. He is anxious to return to England and greatly frustrated by a prescribed stay of at least 40 days in Bordighera while Lucy's leg mends. He is highly suspicious too of Italians: he believes they are all armed either with rosary beads – he is a staunch Protestant – or stilettos. The countryside is, to his mind, barbaric, seething with bandits and republican activists. He had found Rome somewhat tiresome but at least he was able to keep English company of his own class: here in rustic Bordighera he cannot procure any of the comforts a nineteenth century Englishman craves abroad. There is no English tea, the countryside is too rugged for cattle so there is no fresh butter and in any case the locals prefer to use olive oil, and there is no fresh beef – fish, poultry, rabbit and goat meat are the mainstays of local cuisine. Doctor Antonio finds the family accommodation in a rustic inn, named Casa Mattone, and from the first simple but delicious meal there, Sir John will gradually begin to appreciate the food.

Casa Mattone at 22 Via Aurelia, Bordighera.
Ruffini had this house in mind when he wrote Doctor Antonio.
The first English visitors to Bordighera
had all read Doctor Antonio
and many of them walked along the coast road
to see the house for themselves

Accepting Antonio as Lucy's doctor is a different matter. Sir John sends John Ducket to Nice in the hastily repaired carriage: today by car or train we can cover the 60 kilometres from Bordighera to Nice in less than an hour. In 1840 getting to Nice (which was still part of Italy, or rather the Kingdom of Sardinia) was a day's journey, meaning that John was away overnight. When he returned with an English doctor Sir John learnt from this doctor that he already knew Doctor Antonio, and his considerable skill with broken bones, and could recommend no finer person to care for Lucy.

As the story progresses Doctor Antonio gradually gains Sir John's trust and Lucy regains her strength. Once the doctor feels she is well enough to move about he arranges for pillows to be piled into a simple cart and organizes trips into the countryside surrounding Bordighera. Localized descriptions of aromatic lemon groves, scented gardens and waving palm fronds give way now to a wider view of the coast, of terraced olive groves, of villages of rough-hewn stone houses precariously piled higgledy-piggledy on mountainsides and hilltops and of wayside churches and shrines where for centuries travellers have given thanks for a safe journey thus far and prayed for protection along the road ahead.

Lucy is enchanted by these outings and so were Ruffini's readers in Britain. Here was another Italy that no-one had previously dared to explore, but so vivid and passionate was Ruffini's account of his homeland that would-be travellers, muffled up at home and longing for an escape to the sun during the bleak British winters, soon overcame their ingrained fear of bandits, heat, dust and grubbiness and wild revolutionaries. They wanted to see for themselves the sights that the charming Sicilian doctor had shown Lucy, and enjoy the same drives and picnics in the countryside. From its publication in 1855 *Doctor Antonio* quickly became a best seller and the British began to arrive in Bordighera.

Among the early intrepid visitors to venture to the new destination – in 1861- was Lord John Russell, former and future Liberal prime minister of Britain.

He stayed at the newly opened Hotel d'Angleterre, Bordighera's first hotel. In the almost village setting of 1860s Bordighera – the population was then around 1,600 – this hotel, built on a grand scale befitting the class of guests it would host, was a novel source of work for local people. Managed by James Lozeron from Switzerland and his English wife, it quickly became the hub of British life in Bordighera.

From 1863 Anglican church services were held there, with the Reverend Henry Sidebottom arriving by stagecoach from Nice each week until 1864, when the Anglican Bishop of Gibraltar appointed him permanent pastor of the rapidly growing British community in Bordighera.

My 1906 edition of *Baedeker's Northern Italy* states that the hotel charged 7-12 francs (or lira) per day for full board – it was by then one among many winter hotels and guesthouses and no longer the most costly. Today, restyled as Villa Eugenia, it is still a very handsome building painted a warm salmon with white trim.

One of Bordighera's Hotel d'Angleterre's own postcards with the date it was sent (1951) written over the original 193… The magnificent garden in front of the hotel has been cut right back to make way for Via Vittorio Emanuele, he town's main east-west artery.

In 1860s Britain word spread that Bordighera's climate was indeed as pleasant, and the countryside just as attractive as Ruffini had described in *Doctor Antonio*.

Tens of thousands of palms, olive trees and citrus trees grew luxuriantly and the winter temperature seldom fell below 10°C as the mountains behind the town protected it from the chilly north winds. Casa Mattone really did exist, just as Ruffini had described it, on the outskirts of the town (photo below).

*Even today palms (phoenix dactylifera and others)
ominate Bordighera's terraced hillsides
among olives and fruit trees, creating a decidedly
North African landscape.*

More fine hotels were built as the inhabitants of Bordighera embraced the innovative concept of their town becoming a winter resort and a tourist destination. Smaller private guesthouses accommodated less demanding visitors and at the same time British families began to build their own villas, again providing employment for local people. Other winter destinations on the Riviera which had been *colonized* by the British, such as Nice and Cannes, had by the late 1800s become quite crowded and busy, and land there was consequently much more expensive. Ruffini's readers relished the prospect of a less-spoilt, semi-rural environment where land was still relatively cheap: a place which still retained its rustic charm. As their villas, in many cases set in spacious grounds, were built, they established other amenities for a comfortable British existence abroad. In many ways these upper class and often aristocratic and artistic people were perfect visitors. They respected local customs and importantly they followed traditional Ligurian building styles and used local craftsmen and materials.

They sought to be as unobtrusive here as they were at home. They brought their own innate elegance and discretion to the winter community and while they didn't necessarily seek the company of the *Bordigotti* they didn't stand aloof either. However, it is only fair to mention that in buying up large tracts of agricultural land they changed the town's surroundings and economic structure in a way that was not always appreciated. Even by the late 1800s there were voices protesting at the felling for example of centuries-old olive trees: the stirrings of environmental protection. In her books *Here and there in Italy and over the Border*, published in 1893, Linda Villari laments the destruction of palm- olive- and citrus groves. And when Giovanni Ruffini returned to Liguria in the 1880s he was dismayed to find that *Doctor Antonio*'s readers had changed the face of Bordighera beyond recognition.

With the start of the British winter, the season began on the Riviera. From mid-October to mid-May entire households set themselves up in Bordighera. Initially they travelled by train from Calais to Nice and then by coach to Bordighera. When the railway line was extended from Nice to Rome in the early 1870s this journey become considerably less tiresome. Even so, asthmatics, bronchial patients and assorted invalids travelling for the benefit of their health were encouraged not to tire themselves unduly during the journey and overnight stops were often made en-route.

The railway line near Bordighera runs parallel to the coast

A sketch map of Bordighera, drawn by a Miss Goodchild around 1885, shows us some of the families whose villas lined one side of a street running at right angles to the coast road. This lane later become Via Bischoffsheim: today it is Via Vittorio Veneto. Hotel d'Angleterre was on the corner and a short distance along Via Bischoffsheim, on the right hand side of the street, stood (and still stands) Scottish writer George MacDonald's massive Casa Coraggio. Heading inland along the same street Miss Goodchild has noted the villas of the Jamiesons, Mrs Bird, Mrs Patrick and Miss Phelps. At the end of Via Bischoffsheim run the traces of the old Roman road, still named Via Romana. Here the Swiss banker Rafael Bischoffsheim had his villa, as did Messrs Wilde, Leach and Hamilton. A little further west was the Daly family who published the "Journal de Bordighera", a weekly newspaper in English, French and Italian which related the comings and goings of the foreign community until 1930. But these are only some of the British community who had residences along or near these two streets – maybe they were in Miss Goodchild's particular circle. Her own villa isn't indicated – her father was one of Bordighera's four British doctors.

The olive grove on the left hand side of Via Bischoffsheim was bought by Sir Charles Henry Lowe and donated to the town as a public garden in 1902. It is still enjoyed today.

Other gifts which Lowe made to Bordighera include the land for the "Victoria Hall" theatre and the lawn tennis club.
The Bordighera Lawn Tennis Club was the first of its kind in Italy, and opened in 1878. Tennis was fairly new game for the English then – Major Walter Wingfield had demonstrated it to Queen Victoria just a few years before. A plaque on the wall of the tennis club commemorates the arrival of Major Wingfield's *magic crate* – la magica cassa – in October 1878 (photo below).

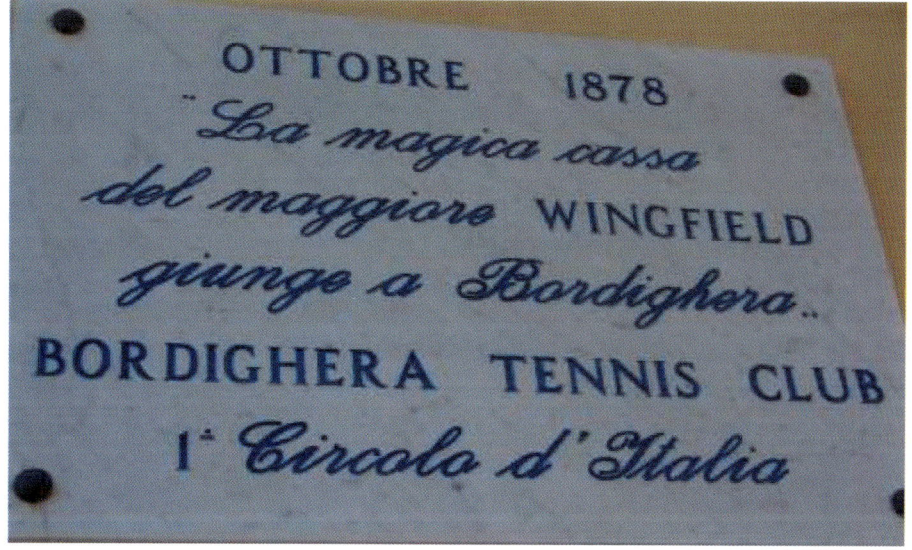

This container was a sort of *DIY tennis court kitset*, providing racquets, balls and nets as well as the game's regulations. Its arrival was no doubt an extremely exciting event and the club expanded rapidly. Situated behind the villas in Via Vittorio Veneto (ex-Bischoffsheim) the BLTC still thrives – as the regular toc-toc-toc and the occasional energetic grunt heard from nearby, even on weekday mornings, testifies. Access to it on foot is from Via Romana down Via dei Tennis (turn right at the bottom into Via Manzoni and follow the BLTC signs) or from Via Vittorio Veneto down Via Shakespeare.

One of the courts with the (ex) Anglican church immediately behind

George MacDonald lived in Bordighera from 1879 to 1902. Here he wrote prolifically as well as holding literary and theatrical events in his imposing villa. Although he died in Britain in 1905 his ashes were later brought back to Bordighera and placed in his wife's grave in the British cemetery there.

Casa Coraggio in Via Vittorio Veneto

MacDonald's neighbours included the Fanshawe family in Villa Rosa: in 1873 Mrs Rosa Fanshawe and her daughter Ellen Rosa, backed financially by Sir Charles Henry Lowe, built a small Anglican church in their back garden, the Anglican community having by now outgrown the hotel rooms where services had been held since 1863. The garden and church, dedicated to All Saints were donated to the British community and the church was enlarged in 1883 and again in 1890. It still stands in its garden setting – deconsecrated but beautifully maintained and used throughout the year as a cultural centre for concerts and exhibitions (photo next page).

All Saints Anglican church, Bordighera

Mrs Fanshawe invited Reverend Clarence Bicknell to be her private chaplain when she built the original little church. Although Bicknell accepted the invitation, after several years in the position he decided to devote his time entirely to the study of the area's flora and natural history. Abandoning his dog collar and donning stout shoes he set out to paint and record Ligurian plants and their habitat. In 1886 he created a museum to house his finds: conferences and meetings were held in the museum's central room and charity plays and concerts were put on there too. The entrance to the museum, just off Via Romana, is enveloped nowadays in a wisteria which flowers gloriously in spring. The staff are extremely knowledgeable and friendly – I always find that once I've negotiated the Morton Bay fig's aerial roots and the drooping wisteria boughs that I have indeed stepped back in time – the more so when I start browsing through the century-old copies of the *Journal de Bordighera*.

Week by week the *Journal* listed all the thousands of foreigners – titled and non – who were in residence in the hotels, guesthouses and private villas and houses. Lords and Ladies, Sirs, Earls and Countesses, Reverends, Barons, Admirals, Colonels and Major Generals: they are all listed with their country of origin along with numerous Mrs., Mr., and Miss, Herr, Frau, Fraulein, Madame, Monsieur and Mademoiselle, Signor and Signora. A truly wonderful multinational mix. The editor invites the residents to send in the names of their guests, and we can imagine that there would have been a fine flurry of sending cards and invitations and receiving visitors. The *Journal* catered primarily for English readers, but articles and advertisements also appeared in French and Italian.

In addition to the publications relating to the British population, if you can't actually make the trip up the Roya valley into the Mercantour National Park, the Bicknell Museum is well worth visiting to view the catalogue Bicknell drew of the Bronze Age rock engravings there.

Views of the Bicknell Museum-Library, Via Clarence Bicknell, off Via Romana, Bordighera

The Moreton Bay fig (ficus magnolioides/macrophylla) which was planted in the museum's garden during its construction has completely overwhelmed the garden's brick fence and a quaint sign on the gate post warns visitors not to linger under the tree.

Views of one of the two monumental Morton Bay figs in the Bicknell Museum-Library's grounds. These trees are both protected: they were planted at the same time as the museum was being built in 1886. The sign says "Don't linger under the Ficus".

In *Doctor Antonio* Sir John Davenne may have lamented the lack of *English* food and comforts during his enforced stay in Bordighera – not so the British community who came to spend their winters here. British butchers, grocery stores, chemists and tearooms vied for their custom along with clothes shops, tailors and milliners. A recipe book was produced in Italian to help the cooks cope with the peculiarities of British cuisine. As well as the English newspapers there were English banks, post and telegraph links to Britain, a British consul, an international library and chess and bridge clubs. There were English doctors and dentists and people offering drawing, sculpting and painting lessons. Just as could have been imagined from Ruffini's descriptions of the local population, Bordighera was an artist's paradise with such picturesque figures as water bearers carrying urns on their heads, fishermen and farmers about their daily tasks, pedlars with trays of colourful wares, impish children and so on. A small school catered for boys and girls. Messrs Woodhouse and Biallie created the town's first electricity company by harnessing the Roya River, and they laid a tramline between Bordighera and Ventimiglia about five miles to the west. In winter the tram ran between Bordighera and Ventimiglia every 15 minutes – just as the buses do today, all year round. A paved waterfront promenade was begun. Again Linda Villari adds a cryptic and critical note in *Here and there in Italy and over the Border*: some British shop keepers in Bordighera don't seem to mind asking their fellow countrymen rather exorbitant prices, and of course bargaining isn't done in a British shop.

With ever improving rail transport the town was easily reached from as far away as Saint Petersburg and the nationalities wintering in the Riviera resort soon included French, Russians, Swiss, Austrians and Germans. As well there were Italians and Americans, so that a truly international community was established, at least each winter from October to May. However, the overwhelming importance of the British contingent is well illustrated in such publications as Dino Taggiasco's *Bordighera* (published in 1930). He dedicates 24 pages to the "Inglesi" – by which we should read "British"! On the other hand, two pages each are devoted to the French – architect Charles Garnier, scientist Louis Pasteur and painter Claude Monet stand out – and to the Germans, where the botanist Ludovico Winter, the painters Federico Von Kleudgen and Hermann Nestel and the poet Viktor Von Scheffel are prominent. Other foreigners – Taggiasco's *Furesti* – are as varied as the Governor of Siberia, the King of Siam and American millionaire Andrew Carnegie.

The winter community's world was not all play – no Victorian colony would have been complete without good works. One of the first people to stand out for her dedication to helping orphans and homeless children was Mrs Louise Boyce. She came to Bordighera as a middle-aged widow in the winter of 1864. As well as her work with the Evangelic Reformed Church and the Waldesians she set up the Boyce Memorial Home in neighbouring Vallecrosia – a boarding school for disadvantaged children, where, along with the gospel they were taught to read and write and the basic skills to help them find work. The colony's rapid expansion meant there was no shortage of work for skilled tradesmen, gardeners, dressmakers, servants and so on. Other generous people created homes for invalids, retired servants and for the elderly. A society for the protection of animals was also established.

On this Linda Villari is full of praise and admiration for the busy women in sensible bonnets and shoes who spend their days helping others. She is very scornful instead of those selfish, hypochondriac women who stayed closed in their hotel lobby, reading the English papers and complaining loudly about Italians and Italian trains. She suggests they would be much better off staying at home for the winter – they don't deserve Bordighera! Interestingly, in *Here and there in Italy and over the Border* Linda Villari is also very dismissive of Ruffini's heroine Lucy Davenne in *Doctor Antonio*. Writing about 35 years after the book was published, she finds Lucy extremely insipid – lacking the spunk and spirit of an 1890s lass. Ruffini and Doctor Antonio are criticized too: although the book had radically altered Bordighera it seems the patriotic sentiments it expressed, and the characters in it, went quite quickly out of vogue once the unification of Italy had taken place.

On 4th April 1882 Queen Victoria, sojourning at the time about 10 miles away in Menton, paid a day visit to Bordighera accompanied by two Carabinieri policeman. Enchanted, she vowed to return. However, nearly twenty years passed before this momentous event could be planned. The date for Her Majesty's stay in Bordighera was set for 1900 and the massive *royal visit machine* was set in motion well in advance. The entire Hotel Angst on Via Romana was booked for the Queen herself – in its advertisements of the time it boasted lifts, electric light, the best sanitary arrangements and steam heating public rooms and passageways. Lodgings were built for the policemen who would accompany the Queen and every villa, hotel and guesthouse in the town was booked in excited anticipation of her visit. However the outbreak of the Boer War made her visit neither safe nor practical. A letter to the editor of the *St James Gazette* of 23rd February 1900, and re-published in the *Journal de Bordighera* a few weeks later commends Her Majesty for deciding against braving the wild and treacherous journey through France to Bordighera – and the risk of being abducted en-route by Kruger's men. Adolf Angst was heartbroken – this visit would have been a great boost to his hotel's fame throughout Europe. Queen Victoria's subjects would have been disappointed too but life went on for them in ever increasing numbers. By 1903 the British winter community out-numbered the Italian population: 3,000 British to just over 2,500 Italians. No other nationality was present in anything like the same numbers.

When World War I broke out many of the town's villas and hotels were turned, at least in part, into hospitals for the wounded and convalescing soldiers from various battle fields around Europe: Hotel Angst alone was able to accommodate 800 of them. Fundraising events took place in aid of the soldiers and as the war ended over 2,000 soldiers returning from European fronts and from India were hospitalized there. An Armistice Day ceremony is still held every year in the British Military Cemetery in Bordighera. (photo below)

Once the war ended the town thrived again as a winter colony and continued to do so until the mid-1930s when the threat of another war strained the relationship between Italy and Britain. Following World War II very few winter *colonists* returned. The villas and many of the grand hotels were turned into blocks of flats.
Hotel Angst stands derelict today in its abandoned garden on Via Romana: a stark, haunting reminder of a glorious past (photo next page). Restoring it will be a massive undertaking and not for the faint-hearted.

Today Bordighera's population stands at around ten and a half thousand. It is a popular beach resort during the summer and during winter its waterfront promenade, Lungomare Argentina, is often crowded with people enjoying the mild climate and sea air. From the tiny Saint Ampelio church in the east, the waterfront stretches west for over two kilometres and joins the waterfronts of neighbouring Vallecrosia and Camporosso.

Bordighera's Lungomare Argentina, looking west from where it begins near St Ampelio church. Cap Ferrat and the Principality of Monaco in the distance left and Menton (France) right. The promenade was named in honour of a visit by Evita Peròn in July 1947, during which she inaugurated the newly repaired walkway, which had been damaged during the war.

How the palm trees came to Bordighera

Palm trees are still a striking feature of the landscape and no account of Bordighera would be complete without a mention of how they came here. In 411 an Egyptian hermit, Ampelio, took refuge in a sea cave on the little promontory at the foot of the headland where Bordighera Alta now stands. He is said to have brought some dates with him when he left Egypt and these grew extremely well in the Ligurian climate. After Ampelio's death in 428 a shine was built over the site of his cave, and he later became Bordighera's patron saint with his feast day on 14th May.

Every year before Easter, Bordighera's palm leaves are sent to the Vatican for the Palm Sunday celebrations. This honour was gained by a local sailor who was among the crowd in Saint Peter's Square in the Vatican on 10th September 1586. After months of preparation an Egyptian obelisk which had been brought to Rome in 39 AD was being hauled upright in the centre of the square. The Pope had warned the crowd of spectators that anyone who made a sound or caused a distraction during this difficult undertaking would be executed. Only when the ropes were beginning to fray and it seemed that the obelisk would crash to the ground, did the daring sailor break the silence. "Water on the ropes!" he cried. Once the obelisk was safely erected the Pope summoned the sailor and thanked him for his timely advice. As a reward he granted Bordighera the right to supply palms to the Vatican.

Prior to Palm Sunday the palm fronds are bound together on the plant to block out the light so that they turn very pale. They are then woven and plaited into intricate shapes which are taken to church to be blessed. These objects are called *parmureli*.

When the British came to winter in Bordighera they loved to go on the outings that Ruffini described when Doctor Antonio took Lucy out to explore her surroundings, and these destinations are just as popular today. Sasso can be reached on foot following well signposted paths from Bordighera Alta. Seborga is an extension of this walk and can also be reached by bus. Dolceacqua and the other villages in the Nervia Valley can be reached by bus. A train from Bordighera will take you to Ventimiglia in the west (and from here into France - towards Nice - and the Principality of Monaco) or to Sanremo, Taggia, Imperia and on to Genoa in the east. Taggia is the closest station to Castellaro and the Sanctuary of Lampedusa.

*At a resort in Arziglia, to the east of Bordighera,
palms grow on the beach,
right down to the shore where they are punctuated
by a plastic replica.*

In Bordighera itself, as well as the places already mentioned – the Bicknell Museum is a must as is a stroll on Lungomare Argentina waterfront and a visit to San Ampelio church – don't miss the villa-museum on Via Romana that was the final home of Italy's first queen, Regina Margherita. Before building Villa Margherita, Queen Margherita had been a guest in the adjacent villa, Villa Etelinda. This gorgeous villa was designed by Charles Garnier for Rafael Bischoffsheim and later sold to Lord Strathmore, the present Queen Elizabeth II's great-grandparents. At the outbreak of World War I Lord Strathmore sold the villa to Regina Margherita.

Finally, spend some time exploring the alleys and piazza's of Bordighera Alta. It is a little gem, an irregular pentagon walled around and laid out exactly as the thirty-two families who decided to move there in 1470 stipulated. These families, at the time living inland a few kilometres away in Borghetto San Nicolò, were mostly farmers and fishermen. They decided to re-build and re-fortify a very ancient settlement on the headland which had been abandoned many centuries before. With sweeping coastal views east and west the new settlement was easier to defend and the air was healthier than inland.

A fresco in Bordighera Alta, showing a sailing gozzo, *a traditional fishing dinghy*

Bordighera Alta, just inside Porta Sottana, the western town gate.

Bordighera Alta – the main square, looking east

References and links
Fiction
Doctor Antonio, John Ruffini, Edinburgh, 1855. My copy is an anastatic reprint by Atene Edizioni, Arma di Taggia, 2000
www.ateneedizioni.com
Non-fiction
Baedekerer's Northern Italy, Leipsic, 1906 – pages 104-107
Bordighera, Armando Besio, Sagep Libri e Communicazione Genova, 1998
Bordighera – Bruckmann's Illustrated Guides no.6 – my copy is a revised bilingual edition produced in "yesterday and today" format by the Bordighera town council in 2009.
Bordighera, Dino Taggiasco, Stabilamento Tipografico Gandolfi 1930
Bordighera e il Museo-Biblioteca dell'Istituto Internazionale di Studi Liguri da Clarence Bicknell al rinnovamento attuale, Istituto Internazionale di Studi Liguri, 1998
The British Colonies in the Italian Riviera in '800 and '900, Alessandro Bartoli, Daner Elio Ferraris Editore srl, 2008.
Here and there in Italy and over the Border, Linda Villari, WH Allen and Co Ltd, London, 1893
Journal et Liste des Estrangers de Bordighera, n.19 and n.20 1900 – I was able to consult these papers which belong to the Fondo Bicknell Istituto Internazionale di Studi Liguri - Bordighera

My special thanks for this ebook go to the very helpful Signora Bruna at Museo Biblioteca Clarence Bicknell and the two fantastic librarians at the International Library's temporary kiosk inside the Tourist Information Office in Via Vittorio Emanuele, Bordighera, the International Library being momentarily closed for renovations.

Bordighera is about 65km from Nice Cote d'Azur airport and about 150 km from Genoa airport. It linked by train to both airports.
www.trenitalia.com for Italian train times, www.voyages-sncf.com for French train times. The French train from Nice will take you to Ventimiglia (Vintimille) where you will change to an Italian train to reach Bordighera.
Local buses around Bordighera www.rivieratrasporti.it
Bordighera town council site www.bordighera.it
Local tourist information www.visitrivieradeifiori.it –
www.rivieradeifiori.com
Museo Biblioteca Clarence Bicknell www.iisl.it
Villa Regina Margherita

www.fondazioneterruzzivillareginamargherita.it

About the author
I'm a New Zealander: I was born in Auckland in the early 1950s. My expat experience began in 1977 when I travelled to the south of Italy by ship. Since then I have lived in Alba, in Piemonte, northern Italy and since 1997 I've been living in a quirky little flat in the ramparts of Ventimiglia Alta, Liguria, north west Italy.
I became interested in writing in 1997 during a period of temporary unemployment. I would like to thank the late Ray Richards of Richards Literary Agency, Auckland, and John Yeoman of The Writers' Village www.writers-village.org for their encouragement and Brian Morris of the New Zealand Institute of Business Studies www.nzibs.co.nz for inspiring me to write ebooks.
I am the author of **"Portraits of the Riviera", Penguin NZ 2004. ISBN 0-14-301911-2.** In "Portraits" I recount my experiences of house-hunting, buying and renovating in Ventimiglia Alta, and take you on excursions into my surroundings – the western Italian Riviera and adjacent French Cote d'Azur and hinterlands.
I've travelled widely throughout Italy and France. I love writing, teaching English, translating and proofreading, travelling and gardening – yes, with two Italian friends I rent a piece of *campagna* where we have an orto (vegetable garden and orchard), barbecues, long, long summer lunches and dinners - and fireflies in spring.

Thank you for your interest in "**How the British came to Bordighera on the Italian Riviera**".

In writing this short ebook I would like to thank all my friends in Italy – Italians and expats – for making my life in your country so pleasant. Without you I might just as well have stayed at home.

If you would like to find out more please contact me by email carolynmckenzie@libero.it

My other ebooks are:
- *Several slightly spooky short stories set on and around the Italian Riviera* http://amzn.to/18RxYgu
- *How to turn your photos into 3D greeting cards* http://amzn.to/1axBD4k
- *The Sanctuary of Our Lady of Virtues – a Miracle, a Pilgrimage and an Easter picnic* http://amzn.to/1bu2Oex
- *An A-Z of Italian street names and the stories they tell of Italian history* http://amzn.to/11I6eZs
- *How to explore Ventimiglia Alta on the Italian Riviera* http://amzn.to/11I5YcK
- *How to Get Ready to Live Your Dream as a Happy Expat in Italy* http://amzn.to/12lkh1X

I am the publisher of *How my Italian adventure began* by Eddie Wise http://amzn.to/1agdgou

In 2012 I assisted my father, Gordon McKenzie, in the e-publication of his childhood memoirs – testimony that you are never too old to embrace modern technology

Blasts from the Past - Tales of a 1930s childhood among Kauri and Kiwi in the far north of New Zealand http://amzn.to/137F5sI

The Gentle Giants - a step back in time in the New Zealand bush to summer 1938 in 3 parts
http://amzn.to/18RAmUl - http://amzn.to/157tXza and http://amzn.to/1b5WNpG

coming soon on facebook – **Ventimiglia Alta Words from the Ramparts and Beyond**

Printed in Great Britain
by Amazon